Contents

Some words are printed in bold, **like this**. You can find out what they mean by looking in the glossary.

What is a team project?

Project planner

Step 1: Write down the project and its requirements.

Step 2: Find out who is on your team.

Step 3: Hold a team meeting.

The class studies different countries in Asia. The teacher assigns a team project – **research** some feature of a specific nation. Karen, Steve, and Claire are on a team for this project, and the country they will research is Thailand.

Types of team projects

Team projects have the same purpose as most other school projects. A team project provides information. The team may decide to **demonstrate** something learned while doing the project, such as a song or dance. Presenting art and music may **persuade** the class to learn more about a subject. If the team makes a presentation at the end of the project, that presentation may also entertain.

Team projects help you develop skills for getting along with people.

ojects

VAL
ES

ojects

nervill

Heinemann
LIBRARY

Heinemann Library is an imprint of Capstone Global Library Limited, a company incorporated in England and Wales having its registered office at 7 Pilgrim Street, London, EC4V 6LB – Registered company number: 6695582

Heinemann is a registered trademark of Pearson Education Limited, under licence to Capstone Global Library Limited

Edited by Nancy Dickmann and Kate DeVilliers
Designed by Richard Parker and Hart McLeod
Picture research by Mica Brancic
Production by Victoria Fitzgerald

Originated by Dot Gradations Ltd
Printed in China by Leo Paper Products Ltd

ISBN 978 0 431931 76 0 (hardback)
13 12 11 10 09
10 9 8 7 6 5 4 3 2 1

ISBN 978 0 431931 81 4 (paperback)
14 13 12 11 10
10 9 8 7 6 5 4 3 2 1

British Library Cataloguing in Publication Data
Somervill, Barbara A.
Team projects. – (School projects survival guides)
371.3'6
A full catalogue record for this book is available from the British Library.

Acknowledgements
We would like to thank the following for permission to reproduce photographs:
© Alamy (Henry Westheim Photography) p. **14**; © Corbis pp. **4**, **18** (David Ashley), **26**; © Getty Images pp. **8** (Photodisc/Stuart Gregory), **20** (PhotoAlto/Laurence Mouton); © Punchstock (ImageSource) p. **24**.

Note paper design features with permission of © istockphoto.com.

Every effort has been made to contact copyright holders of material reproduced in this book. Any omissions will be rectified in subsequent printings if notice is given to the publishers.

There are, however, major differences between an individual project and a team project. The obvious difference is working with other pupils, which is also a learning experience. Team projects are also larger in scope than individual projects because they show the work of several people.

Teams are different

If you are not used to working on a team, you may have many questions about what to do. What exactly does working on a team involve? How will your team be organized? Can you choose your team or will your teacher select the team? These are good questions to ask, and your teacher will have the answers.

Regardless of how the team is chosen, you will have to work well with others. This skill of getting along with other people will last your entire life. There are few jobs or social situations where people work totally alone. Think of your team as you would a sports team. On a football team, you cannot play striker, defender, and goalie at the same time. To win, all team members must know and play their positions. A team project works the same way. Team members have jobs and responsibilities.

Questions to ask your teacher

You will want to know the answers to these and other questions before starting your project:

- How is the team organized?
- How much time will we have to work on this project in class?
- If we have to do a presentation, can we use classroom equipment or do an experiment?
- Will the team have computer access for research and writing?
- Will we have time to work in the library?
- What should we do if someone on the team does not do his or her work?
- How will the team be marked?

Understand the project

Everyone on your team must understand what the project includes and how much work needs to be done. What is the subject area? How long do you have to do the work? What are the requirements of the project?

At the start, your team needs time to work together and plan your project. There will be work you do together, but team members will also have specific jobs to do on their own. You need to meet several times during the project period to discuss the progress the team is making.

As the teacher explains the project fully, you should take notes. For the project on Thailand, the team must produce a written report, a display of some type, a list of **resources** used, and a presentation to the class. Your project might require something different.

The teacher also reads off the list of teams. You might find yourself on a team you would not normally choose. That is fine as long as you go into the project with a positive attitude. The best team is one made up not of close friends but of hard workers. Begin with the idea that your teammates bring different knowledge, ideas, and skills to the project. Believe that they – and you – will work hard.

Holding a meeting

When you work with others, it is very important to get a good start. Hold your first team meeting as soon as you can. At the meeting, you share contact information (phone numbers, email addresses) so you can keep in touch after school or on weekends.

This is a good time to find out what demands team members have on their time besides school. One might be on a sports team. Another member might have to practise a musical instrument. You will all have outside activities that must be considered when planning the project.

Take notes at the team meeting. Write down main ideas and agreements presented during any meeting. At the next meeting, begin by reviewing those notes.

Make a schedule

Make a project schedule that includes everyone's time issues. Do not forget that this project will not be the only thing you have to do for school. Build homework and studying time into your schedule. A planner for a group is much more difficult than one you make for your own use. While making up the schedule, your team should also commit to time during the week to work on the project.

Make a schedule that lists when each team member can work on the project. Here is an example of a one-week schedule:

	Monday	Tuesday	Wednesday	Thursday	Friday	Weekend
In class	Project time		Project time	Project time		
After school						
Claire	Football	Project time	Project time	Guitar	Football	Project time
Karen	Project time	Piano	Drama club	Piano	Project time	Project time
Steve	Rugby	Project time	Rugby	Project time	Project time	Project time

CHAPTER CHECKLIST

✓ We know how team projects are different.
✓ We understand the project.
✓ We have a project schedule.

Choosing a project

During their first meeting, Karen, Steve, and Claire **brainstorm** ideas for a topic. Their project is Thailand, but what feature of Thailand? Steve suggests sports and music. Karen wants to study Thai theatre or art. Claire's idea is a make-believe trip through Thailand. The team talks about each topic. Finally, they settle on the title of their project: "The Arts of Thailand".

Brainstorming ideas

A brainstorming session gives every team member an opportunity to offer ideas. As each person offers ideas, one team member should take notes. Then, the team can discuss each idea. One positive aspect of brainstorming is that suggested topics probably interest the team. You will produce a better project studying a topic that interests all team members.

For a team project, there are at least two areas to talk about. The first is what topic the team will research. Review all possible topics suggested by the team. On a project about a country, topics might include art, music and dancing, history, government, or geography. The second area for discussion is how to handle the topic. Make sure that whatever your team plans meets the assignment given by the teacher.

Claire, Karen, and Steve decide to study the art of Thailand. The unique art of Thailand can be seen throughout the country.

Before your team commits to a topic, do some **pre-research** in the library. Find out if there is enough research material available on your possible topic to support a team project.

Expanding or narrowing a topic

The project topic you choose must be broad enough to provide tasks for every team member. Think about the Thai arts topic. Suppose your team narrowed the topic to just Thai pottery. That probably would not provide enough work for all team members. By expanding the areas covered by the topic, your teammates will all have work to do.

Teammates should select the **sub-topics** they wish to study. Pick topics in rounds until all topics are covered. For each round, a different teammate should pick first. In that way, you will all have made choices that suit your interests.

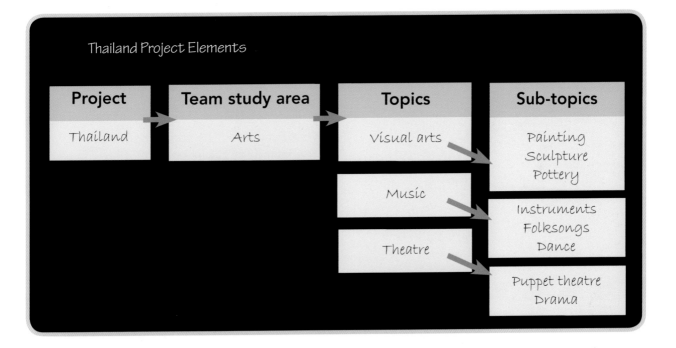

Thailand Project Elements

Project	Team study area	Topics	Sub-topics
Thailand	Arts	Visual arts	Painting Sculpture Pottery
		Music	Instruments Folksongs Dance
		Theatre	Puppet theatre Drama

CHAPTER CHECKLIST

✓ We brainstormed topics.
✓ We chose a topic broad enough to provide tasks for all.
✓ We took turns selecting sub-topics to research.

Working with a team

Project planner

Step 1: Learn the role of a team leader.

Step 2: Know what makes a successful team.

Step 3: Identify team talents.

The team is having problems getting started. They cannot seem to make any decisions, and their discussions go in all different directions. The team needs a leader and some directions on what to do. The team asks the teacher how to get organized.

Getting started

It is important for your team to have a leader. The leader is not a "boss" and does not tell everyone what to do. Consider a school team leader like a sports team captain. A good captain helps others get organized and encourages teammates. You need to choose one team member to be the leader. If you are team leader, you must find a way to make everyone on the team feel useful.

Your leader guides the team meetings. The leader might take notes of what goes on at the meeting or set up the schedule. However, you want teammates to participate in all aspects of planning. Teammates should feel free to offer suggestions, disagree with the leader, and also recommend any changes.

TEAMBUILDERS

Communicating with others requires both talking and listening. Make sure you tell your teammates your ideas, but you also need to listen to other teammates' ideas.

Handling criticism

There are two types of **criticism**: **constructive** and negative. Constructive criticism improves the project while making people feel good about their work. Negative criticism is making nasty, unpleasant comments about other people or their work. Negative criticism rarely produces positive results. Criticism should always be positive. Never say, "That's stupid." Try: "Let's see how we might make that idea work."

Elements of a successful team

Coordinating the work

A large project is like a difficult recipe. It has many ingredients and many steps for putting it together. Define the elements and work them into a plan you can all live with.

Constant communicating

Talk to each other about project work, problems, and deadlines. Be open and honest with your team about your feelings about the project.

Cooperating with each other

Make sure you work together to reach goals. Getting along with each other is as much a part of a team project as doing the writing or artwork.

Criticizing constructively

When you make a comment about someone else's work, make it positive. Say, "That's an interesting idea. How can we make it work?" You can improve on an idea without hurting other people's feelings.

Successful team meetings

There are several basic actions that make a team successful. Teams need to communicate. Every team member looks at a project differently, and each person's opinions are valuable. As you discuss the project, you can get new ideas about how to produce the work needed. When you talk, be respectful of other people's feelings.

The talk among team members should be positive, even when it **criticizes** someone's work. Suppose the team is doing research, but one team member does not finish on time. Yelling will not help. You might say, "You did well on the first part, but you need to finish. When do you think that can happen?" You usually get a better answer with a positive approach.

What makes a successful meeting? If your team is not careful, your meetings might get out of hand. You may spend too much time meeting and too little time producing results. A successful meeting has goals and a plan, called an **agenda**. It is the team leader's job to make sure everyone sticks to the plan.

HELPFUL HINT!

In a team meeting, pay attention while others are talking and listen to their ideas. You will have time to speak, so wait for your turn. Interrupting others wastes team time.

Here is an example. Today's meeting has three aims. The team needs to assign research topics, fill out the project calendar, and set **deadlines**. The team leader opens the meeting by telling other members what the team will be discussing. This is not a speech or a list of orders. Instead, the leader should encourage everyone to take part in the discussion.

Teammates should make regular reports on how their assigned tasks are progressing. If a problem comes up, tell the team immediately. Everyone has emergencies, and you will too. These problems can be handled if the team understands why you need help.

Get the most out of your team – respect the ideas and opinions of others.

Identifying team talents

The ideal team project has everyone participating on an equal level. That means that all teammates do roughly an equal amount of research, an equal amount of writing, and have equal roles in presenting the material. The problem with dividing the material so exactly is that it does not allow for people's talents.

One teammate might be a good artist. Another might write well or speak well. In one of your early meetings, ask teammates what they feel might be their best contributions to the project. Accept that you cannot do the entire project yourself – and you should not do it all. If you did, you would soon **resent** your teammates. If you learn to appreciate the work others do, you will feel better about your team project.

CHAPTER CHECKLIST

- ✓ We chose a team leader.
- ✓ We held successful team meetings.
- ✓ We recognized each other's talents.

Making choices together

Project planner

Step 1: Determine the exact elements of your project.

Step 2: Break the project into tasks.

Step 3: Assign tasks.

After doing some research, the team decides to make a **mural** of Thai arts and entertainment. The mural will be part of the presentation required for the project. Karen, Steve, and Claire divide up the research and set a deadline for getting it done. Claire is a better artist, but Steve is a better writer. Karen's experience with drama club makes her the natural choice for lead presenter.

A mural is one way to show special elements of Thai art.

Time, talent, and money

Your team project must have limits. You cannot produce a project that takes months to complete because you have limited time. You cannot produce an original piece of music if no team member has musical talent. And, you cannot choose a project that costs a great deal of money. Keep your project under control. When you know what you cannot do, it is easier to plan a project that you can do.

Look back at the project. What does your teacher want? The project elements are the items your teacher asked for when the assignment was made. Discuss ways the team can fulfill the assignment.

Money is also something to think about. Do not plan anything that will cost large amounts of money. You may need some supplies, and you should share the costs of those supplies. If you have some materials you can contribute, then do so. For instance, a team chooses to provide different foods from India, the nation it is studying. When the team looks into the cost, it is too expensive. Teammates decide instead to just make an Indian bread called *nan* or *naan*.

Breaking the project into tasks

A good team project has everyone participating at all levels of the project. Once you pin down the project elements, you need to break each element into individual tasks. This should be a team effort.

Research, for example, is a major task that should be broken down into smaller units. Research takes time, and everyone can help. Have the team brainstorm every sub-topic that needs to be researched. Review the list together and divide it into two, three, or four sub-topics per team member. Work out how much time you need to spend on the research for each topic. Make sure you limit the number of topics researched to match the time you have available.

Assign the project elements

Most people will work very hard on a task that they choose. They will not work as well on a task they do not want to do. Your teammates will produce better work if they volunteer for specific tasks.

Try to find a way for each teammate to do an equal amount of work without being too strict. Make sure that team members are comfortable completing their parts. This does not mean that one person should do all the writing or all the speaking. Just try to balance talents with the project elements.

Some parts of the project will be fun. Other parts may be less enjoyable. All team members should share in the fun aspects. Likewise, everyone should work on the more difficult parts. Every teammate needs to do at least some of each project element.

Commitments

You need to understand that people work at different paces. When assignments are made, each team member must agree to meet project deadlines. A deadline is the time by which something must be done or completed. Try your best never to miss a deadline, but you should understand that emergencies do come up.

While you cannot control what other team members do, you can control yourself. To meet your deadline on time, get a good start. When you put your work off to the last minute, problems may pop up. You might get sick, have to go to the dentist, or a family emergency may occur. Avoid such problems by starting immediately. You do not want to tell your team that you did not get your work done.

Make a chart that lists each team member's project commitments. Here is an example:

Thai arts and entertainment	Claire	Karen	Steve
Research Deadline: _____	Sculpture Pottery Dance	Painting Musical instruments Drama	Films Folksongs Puppet theatre
Writing Deadline: _____	• 2–3 paragraphs on each research topic	• 2–3 paragraphs on each research topic • Proofreading	• 2–3 paragraphs on each research topic • Edit and put together writing into one unified paper
Display material Deadline: _____	• Design mural • Paint mural	• Help paint mural	• Help paint mural
Presentation Deadline: _____	• Discuss three research topics	• Narrator • Discuss three research topics	• Discuss three research topics

CHAPTER CHECKLIST

✓ We broke the project into smaller sections.
✓ We assigned sections fairly.
✓ We all agreed to meet section deadlines.

Researching together

Project planner

Step 1: Plan a trip to the library.

Step 2: Work together to find material.

Step 3: Take notes for all to use.

Karen, Steve, and Claire meet at the library. They are going to try to do the research together. That is one way to make sure that the team gets its research done. They could do all their work separately, but that is not the purpose of a team project. If you are truly going to be a team, do as much of your work together as you can.

Visit the library

You are at the library, so talk to the expert. Ask the librarian for help in finding research on your topic. Librarians know where everything is and can help you get a solid start. Set up at a table and collect all the books you can find on your topic. Review for all sub-topics and share books that have material your teammates might use.

Research your topic using the **OPAC**. You can search by subject, author, or title. When you search by subject, try as many substitutes for the topic as you can think of. For example, Steve's team might look for Thailand, oriental arts, Asian arts, Asian music, and oriental theatre.

You may work together or individually to find your research material.

Surf the Internet

You may also work as a team doing research on the computer. Make a list of topics your team needs to look up. Divide the list up so that each teammate has information to look up.

HELPFUL HINT! Bring a pack of small sticky notes with you to the library. As you find material for you or your teammates, mark it with a note.

If you are using a school or library computer, you need to ask about printing pages you find. There may be a limit on printing so that paper and ink are not wasted. If so, you will need to take notes. Make sure you go through all of the topics on the team's list so there is enough research to use for your report.

The material you collect needs to be accurate and reliable. When looking on the Internet, use websites that end with .edu, .org, or .gov, in their web addresses. These addresses stand for colleges, universities, museums, government agencies, and other such groups. Their information is usually factual, up-to-date, and ideal for research in comparison to websites that end in .com.

After your team finishes researching, it may be helpful to sort all of the notes and information by using a **planning tool**. Different planning tools work well for different types of information. You can find examples of useful planning tools on the Internet. Use a **search engine** and enter "planning tool".

CHAPTER CHECKLIST
- ✓ We found good books to use.
- ✓ We did research on the Internet.
- ✓ We used reliable sources.

Team troubles

Project planner

Step 1: Identify problems.

Step 2: Hold a meeting.

Step 3: Ask for help.

The team is in trouble. The project is due on Friday, and the team is worried that they will not be done in time. Karen, Steve, and Claire each have excuses for what has gone wrong, but excuses do not get the project done. It is time to ask their teacher what to do.

Recognizing problems

Working together can be a challenge. The same things that make teamwork interesting – different approaches, ideas, and talents – can also lead to problems. Teams struggle with poor use of time, people not getting along, and failed **communication**.

To keep your team on track, meet often to talk about both progress and problems. Be calm when talking, particularly about the problems. Ask everyone to offer solutions to whatever is going wrong. Team problems are shared problems. The solutions must be shared also.

Some team projects can be frustrating. Try to work out solutions to any problems that come up.

Asking for help

Do not wait until the last minute to ask for help. If the team needs help, get it straight away. You might need your teacher to talk to the team if problems are not being solved. Remember, you are part of a team. The solutions to problems need to be worked out as a team, not as individuals.

Sorting out team problems

Problem	Possible solutions
Not getting along together	You may often work with people you do not like. Think about the project and work. Put aside your differences – you do not need to be friends to work together.
Work is not getting done on time	Ask why the work is not getting done. Listen – there may be a good reason. For good reasons, such as illness, work out how you can all help. Revise the work schedule. For laziness, ask the teacher for help.
Poor communication	Talk and listen. Share information. Find ways to help each other.
Poor attitudes, bossiness, bad feelings	Talk about the situation in a positive way. Discuss what changes can be made by saying, "We should…" not "You should…" Never accuse or abuse other teammates. Encourage others by using praise.
Unbalanced work load	One teammate makes a point of doing too little work, forcing another to do too much. This is not fair and should be handled by the teacher.

CHAPTER CHECKLIST

✓ We resolved problems.
✓ We talked and listened.
✓ We asked for help.

Putting it all together

Project planner

Step 1: Write, revise, and edit your writing.

Step 2: Produce a final draft.

Step 3: Create a display.

The research is done, but there is still plenty to do to complete the project. At a meeting, the team creates a quick outline for the required written report. They also talk about the mural and project presentation. The team decides that team members will write rough drafts of the material they researched. One team member will compile the material into the final report.

Writing and editing

Writing is basically an individual task. That does not mean that the team should not work together on writing their report. Here is one way to write together. Teammates begin by creating an outline of the report together. The outline gives the order for the written material.

Basic elements of a written report

Review the project to make sure you are providing the materials required. Here is a list of elements frequently found in a written report:

- Cover
- Table of contents
- **Introduction, body**, and **conclusion**
- Illustrations, maps, charts, or graphs
- A list of reference materials

Next, teammates write up the material they researched themselves. Develop each topic on a separate page. The pages are then put in order according to the outline. Now, the individual work begins. One team member reviews and edits all the writing. That person smoothes out the written matter, creating a report that flows from topic to topic. Another teammate can put together the list of **references**. These are the articles, books, and other materials used to produce the project. Your teacher can tell you the format needed for listing reference materials.

Once the first draft is finished, other teammates can help again. They can proofread for grammar, spelling, and punctuation errors. The teammate with the best handwriting should copy the entire report into a final draft. Some teachers may require the report to be printed from a computer. If so, decide who will type up the final report.

Creating displays

Often, a group project will require a display of some kind. A display may be a poster, a mural, a **diorama**, model, or map. An experiment or demonstration might support a report on a science topic.

As the writer is working on the report, other teammates should work on the other project parts. If the display is supposed to support the report, it needs to have an obvious connection. For example, a mural or collage of Thai arts would be good visual support for a report on that topic. Make sure you label your display and provide a large, readable headline.

CHAPTER CHECKLIST

✓ We worked on the report together.
✓ We produced a final draft.
✓ We planned a display or demonstration.

Finishing up

Project planner

Step 1: Create a presentation.

Step 2: Give positive feedback.

Step 3: Review what you learned.

The team practises their presentation. "In Thailand," Karen begins, "art, music, and theatre link the old and the new. Ancient statues hold up the palaces of kings, and young girls paint traditional scenes on umbrellas." As Karen gives a general overview of Thai arts and entertainment, Steve and Claire point out highlights on their team mural. All of the teammates take part in the presentation.

An oral presentation

If you need to make an oral presentation, you should work together to decide what you want to say and the order in which you say it. Your team should have an announcer or narrator, but every teammate needs to play a part. It would be best for you to talk about the information you researched yourself because you know it better than your teammates.

If you have to do a presentation, plan some time for a practice session.

If you have several people involved, you need to create a script. Your script does not need to be exact, but it does need to note who speaks when. Practise your part on your own, and then get your team together for a practice session. It is best to practise in front of an audience. Ask that person to make constructive comments.

Presentations can be simple or your team can create something unusual. To do so, mix what is popular among your friends with the topic that you are studying. Here is an alternative suggestion for the Thai art project. The team could create a magazine about Thai arts and entertainment that they hand out to the class. Articles might have included a pretend interview with a Thai puppeteer, a review of Thai parasol painting, and ads for various entertainment events. These articles are written based on research available.

TEAMBUILDERS

Be enthusiastic and supportive. When the project is finished, look over it and say, "We did a great job!"

Handling nerves

Most people suffer an attack of nerves, or stage fright, before making a presentation. There are several aids to help you get those shaky knees under control. Begin by doing your work and practising before the presentation. If you know your material, you will not be as nervous.

Take three deep breaths and think about relaxing just before you speak. Go over your notes one last time. Then, tighten and loosen your fists or give your legs a quick stretch. Finally, see yourself giving a successful presentation in your mind. If you see success, you will be a success.

The big event

Your team project is at an end. It does not matter whether the end is a written report or presentation. Make one last review to be sure you have fulfilled the project requirements.

If you are handing in a written report, it should be as neat as possible. A display should be attractive, labelled, and easily read from a distance. Your presentation should cover all aspects of the assignment and be interesting to the audience. If you meet the assignment requirements, you have done all you can. Be happy with the results.

HELPFUL HINT!

When you hand in your report, you need to put the names of all teammates on the cover. List the names in alphabetical order to avoid problems.

What did you learn?

Your final team meeting should take place after the project ends. You should discuss what you have learned. The written report received an excellent mark. Your teacher also liked the display your team made. Those were team successes.

Unfortunately, your presentation was not very well organized. Your team did not practise as much as it should have. That part of the project was less successful. Plus, your teacher felt you needed to use more reference materials for your presentation.

As a group, ask yourselves what could have been done better. This is not a time to point fingers but to point out how to improve on the next team project. There will be more team projects throughout your life.

Make sure you celebrate the completion of your team project.

You have also learned individual lessons. First of all, you learned all the information about your project topic. You have also learned how to work together with others. This is not easy, and even adults sometimes have problems working together. You have learned to respect others, communicate better, and listen to the opinions of others.

When dealing with people, you might also consider what you personally would do differently. You might find better ways to talk to your teammates. If you did not talk openly, you will want to voice your ideas. You may have enjoyed earning praise, and you should have become more comfortable giving praise.

The most important aspect of teamwork is friendship. By working with other people you might make a new friend. Your new social skills will work at home, with teams or clubs, and with your friends. Team projects not only teach you how to be a good teammate, but also how to be a better person.

CHAPTER CHECKLIST

✓ We finished on time.
✓ We learned how to work together.
✓ We succeeded as a team.

Project Ideas

These projects can work for nearly any class subject. The examples given can be a starting point for you to develop your team project.

You are there – eyewitness to XXX

This is a sketch in which your team pretends to be at an event. You might use this project idea to describe Marco Polo's trip to China, the discovery of penicillin, or the events that led to writing *The Lion, The Witch, and the Wardrobe*.

In the news

This would be a news broadcast as though it came from a specific time period. Possibilities might be a series of reports on events connected to World War II or an element of science, such as volcanoes.

Interview with XXX

Similar to a news broadcast, this would be an interview between a reporter and a famous person, such as Elizabeth I, Michelangelo, or William Shakespeare. The reporter could also interview others who have been affected by the famous person, such as an actor in Shakespeare's group.

If we lived in XXX

Like time travel, your team may transport itself back to another time or to a place far from home. The team might present a discussion of what it would be like if you lived in ancient Egypt or modern-day Thailand.

The XXX Times

Write your own team newspaper or magazine. Most topics would fit this project idea, but it does work best with history or social studies projects. Write about the event as if it were happening at the moment.

The amazing event

The explorations of a distant land, the discovery of planets or new medicines, or a major event in history are ideal for this project. Your team could produce a diary of the situations that led up to the event. For example, your team studies the journey of Christopher Columbus, and each teammate creates a diary with eight entries from the point of view of different people on the trip: Columbus, a crewman, and a captain of one of the vessels.

The incredible XXX

Take a trip through time and create an advertising campaign to promote a new invention, medical discovery, or idea. You might convince people to immigrate to the colonies or use that newfangled telephone.

Dear diary

Do you keep a diary? Do you think famous people did? Imagine that you are King John, and the other nobles want you to sign the Magna Carta. Pretend you are Mary Seacole, and you are travelling to the Crimea to help nurse wounded soldiers. Each night you write in your diary. What do you say? That's for you and your teammates to decide.

Everyday heroes

Have you ever considered people who are everyday heroes? These people might be doctors, firefighters, teachers, or parents. They might be ordinary people who did extraordinary things, such as saving someone's life. People who gather clothing for the homeless, or work to save endangered species are also everyday heroes. Present their stories in a sketch, written report, or mock television programme.

Research resources

In the library

Almanacs

An almanac is published every year. It contains facts, figures, and statistics on many different topics. Make sure you use the most recent edition to get current facts.

Atlases

An atlas is a book of maps, usually covering the entire world. Additional maps may show the oceans, ocean currents, agriculture, how land is used, and population.

Dictionaries

Most dictionaries do more than just give definitions of words. Standard dictionaries may contain **synonyms**, **antonyms**, usage, word origin, and pronunciation. There are also biographical and geographical dictionaries available.

Encyclopaedias

An encyclopaedia contains information on a wide variety of subjects. There are also narrower versions, such as an encyclopaedia of mammals, sports, plants, and so on.

School or public librarians

When doing research you should first talk to a librarian. Librarians know how to find information and how to get that information for you.

On the Internet

Homework help

There are many sites that offer help with homework. The BBC Schools site – www.bbc.co.uk/schools – has help on all the primary subjects.

Internet Public Library

The Internet Public Library (www.ipl.org) is like having a library on your computer. You can search through the site for information on geography, science, literature, history, and so on. You can read a book, a magazine, or a newspaper.

Online news

Most major newspapers, news magazines, and television stations have news websites. Many have search windows. Enter your topic and click "search".

Search engines

Search engines have many interesting names – Ask.com, Google, and Yahoo, to name a few. Each of these search engines works in the same way. Enter a topic in the search window, click, and the engine finds articles and websites that fill your request. Be patient. You may not find what you need on the first attempt.

Glossary

agenda schedule of discussion topics or events for a meeting

antonym word that means the opposite of another word

body main section of a speech or written piece

brainstorm come up with quick ideas on a topic

communication the act of talking and listening between people

conclusion end of a speech or written piece

constructive positive, or designed to build or create

criticism spoken or written comments that judge the work of another person

criticize comment on or point out errors or faults

deadline time by which a project or part of a project must be completed

demonstrate show how something is done or how something works

diorama three-dimensional representation of a scene, such as those seen in museums

introduction opening of a speech or written piece

mural large picture painted onto a wall or large poster that is displayed on a wall

OPAC (Online Public Access Catalogue) tool for finding library materials by author, title, or subject

persuade convince someone

planning tool visual aid for sorting information

pre-research look into a topic before beginning the actual project

reference source of information

research look up information about a subject; the information itself

resent feel anger towards a person

resource place to find information, such as a book or magazine article

search engine program on the Internet designed to find articles and websites on specific topics

sub-topic lesser topic, one that falls under a larger, major category

synonym word with the same or similar meaning, such as "home" and "house"

Index